CONFIDENT

CONFIDENT

50 MINDFULNESS AND RELAXATION EXERCISES

TO BOOST YOUR SELF-ESTEEM

Dr. Arlene Unger
and Lona Eversden

METRO BOOKS
New York

METRO BOOKS
New York

An Imprint of Sterling Publishing Co., Inc.
1166 Avenue of the Americas
New York, NY 10036

This book is not intended as a substitute for medical or
psychotherapeutic advice, and readers are advised to consult a healthcare
professional for individual concerns and to check that the exercises are
suitable for their particular needs. The creators of the work and the
publisher cannot be held liable for any actions that may be taken as
a consequence of the information in this book.

ISBN 978-1-4351-6444-4

For information about custom editions, special sales,
and premium and corporate purchases, please contact Sterling
Special Sales at 800-805-5489 or specialsales@sterlingpublishing.com.

Manufactured in China by Toppan Leefung Printers Limited

2 4 6 8 10 9 7 5 3 1

www.sterlingpublishing.com

Credits
Publisher: Kerry Enzor
Co-author: Lona Eversden
Project Editor: Anna Southgate
Designer: Dave Jones
Senior Editor: Philippa Wilkinson
Production Manager: Zarni Win

CONTENTS

INTRODUCTION

Confidence and courage come from within. They are states of mind, epitomized by a belief that you have some value, by a sense of comfort in your body, and by a conviction that you can succeed. When you believe you are worthwhile, you convey this to others, and studies show that when people feel good about themselves, they get treated in ways that further boost their self-esteem.

There is plenty of research to suggest that being confident of success can become a self-fulfilling prophecy: It makes success more likely. Why? Because when you believe in yourself, you tackle challenges with less anxiety and are more able to focus. That focus leads to greater competence and gives you the wins that further fuel your courageous instincts. In short, confidence and courage are tools to help you live the life you want and realize your potential. They mean letting go of fears and worries that hold you back; they mean having the ability to know what you want, whatever others say. If you have confidence in yourself, you can face the world with courage in your heart, and this can benefit your work, your home life, and your relationships in many ways.

Being confident doesn't mean that you never doubt yourself. But the key thing about confident people is that they do not allow their fears to control what they do—they cultivate bravery and choose action over inaction. And even when things go wrong, confident people bounce back better from setbacks and don't let these dent their feelings of self-worth—they are always ready to start again.

The enemies of confidence

Low self-confidence can often be deep-rooted in our experience of childhood, or may be the result of illness or events that we experience in adulthood. Fear, self-doubt, self-criticism, shame, and perfectionism can all undermine our confidence. Unfortunately low self-confidence can make it seem that there are dangers and pitfalls at every turn. When we feel this way, we often elect to avoid challenging situations, but this can serve to confirm our feeling that we do not have a place in the world, and so prevent us from making the most of opportunities that come our way.

Although it may seem that some people are naturally confident, every one of us can work to enhance our confidence levels. In this book you will find 50 short exercises that you can practice regularly in order to do just that. They draw on compelling psychological research, techniques of visualization and affirmation, and the therapies of cognitive behavioral therapy (CBT), emotional brain training (EBT), and mindfulness-based stress reduction (MBSR).

Emotional brain training

This approach, sometimes abbreviated to EBT, is based on the idea that our natural stress response becomes wired into the "emotional brain." It teaches that we can identify our state of mind at any given moment and use the brain's natural pathways to direct it away from stress. It offers a toolkit of skills that foster greater authenticity and self-acceptance, encourage clarity of purpose, and boost our ability to relate to others, all of which build confidence. It also emphasizes the need for a positive healthy lifestyle.

When to seek help

We can all improve our confidence through self-help measures such as the ones in this book. But if your emotional issues are continual or they impact on your everyday life, work, or relationships, you should consult your family physician or a professional therapist for individual advice and support.

TEN **BENEFITS** OF **CONFIDENCE**

1 Enables you to say "no" to others.

2 Inspires you to take on challenges and stretch yourself.

3 Lets you embrace uncertainty.

4 Endows you with resilience, so that you can bounce back from setbacks.

5 Helps you know your strengths, so that you can make the most of them.

6 Increases your ability to accept your flaws, and those of others too.

7 Encourages you to meet others, socialize, and stay connected.

8 Reduces regrets and "what ifs."

9 Gives you the ability to speak in public.

10 Impresses others and helps them believe in you.

How to use this book

This book shows you how to raise your confidence levels through a variety of methods and psychological techniques. You can open the book at random and practice the exercise you find, or you can make this a more long-term project, working through the chapters chronologically. Seize the day and get started right away.

Cognitive behavioral therapy

This therapy—CBT for short—is used to treat a wide range of issues, including low self-esteem, depression, and anxiety. It looks at how we think, the ways in which our thoughts form the basis of our actions and feelings, and how, in turn, our actions can affect the way we think and feel. In cognitive behavioral therapy, we learn how to identify and challenge negative automatic thoughts that can undermine our self-esteem and lead us to behave in unhelpful and self-defeating ways. We can then replace them with more positive ones.

Mindfulness-based stress reduction

Mindfulness is a way of living in the present, rather than being distracted by worries over past actions or anxiety about the future. Mindfulness-based stress reduction (MBSR) encourages us to pay full attention to our experience of breathing, feelings, thoughts, bodily sensations, and our surroundings. This focused awareness is known to help regulate our emotion and boost our capacity for happiness. It can also help with self-esteem, because it teaches us to recognize and let go of self-limiting criticisms and judgments. Mindfulness practice is known to improve our ability to concentrate, so it can help us become more productive, thus increasing our effectiveness and—in time—belief in our abilities.

Visualizations

There's a large body of research to show that acting as if you already possess a certain attribute can actually help you to feel it. The "as if" tool is used in modern sports psychology to help athletes visualize themselves succeeding before an important race or match in order improve their confidence and prepare themselves for the real thing. Science has shown that rehearsing an outcome can have a deep-rooted effect on our minds and bodies. One experiment showed that skiers imagining themselves skiing downhill created neural firings in their muscles that were almost the same as when they skied in real life. You can use this technique in the same way when preparing yourself to give a presentation, to go to a party, or to boost your confidence in doing almost anything.

Affirmations

Short statements intended to send a positive message to the brain and encourage confident thinking, affirmations are another "as if" technique. They are used in cognitive behavioral therapy and feature in exercises throughout the book.

Science has shown that when we visualize ourselves doing an activity, our bodies respond in similar ways to when we do that same activity in reality. Visualization is a powerful tool that we can use to boost our self-confidence and courage.

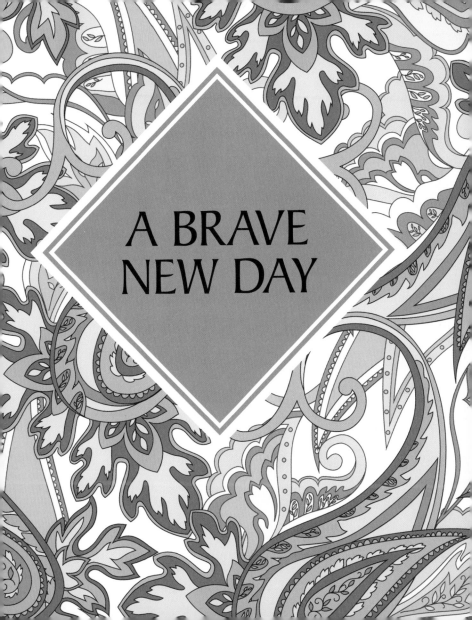

A BRAVE
NEW DAY

Confidence is not a static personality trait that you either have or don't have. It's something that is within all of us, and that we can access at any point in our lives. Furthermore, confidence is something that you can work on and develop. This chapter introduces some of the easy, achievable steps you can introduce to your daily routine in order to boost your courage, little by little.

Some of these techniques are psychological methods. Research shows that simply altering the way you stand can create a surge of self-confidence. You can also boost your confidence through turbo-charging your lifestyle. Exercising more, improving your sleep patterns, eating healthy foods, and getting more natural light—these are all known to increase positivity and foster confidence.

You can visualize your way to greater confidence, simply by imagining a braver you. All the exercises in this chapter are based on scientific research or draw on the therapies of cognitive behavioral therapy, emotional brain training, and mindfulness practice.

RADIATE WITH LIGHT

For an easy extra boost of confidence, be sure to get enough daylight. Sunlight helps us to produce serotonin, the brain chemical that governs happiness and self-esteem. Try this empowering exercise to kickstart your morning and remind yourself to increase the light factor in your day.

1 When you get up in the morning, open your curtains or blinds and look out at the daylight. If your bedroom isn't brightly lit, go to a sunnier room to do the exercise.

2 Looking out of the window, breathe in deeply and raise your arms straight above your head. Breathing out, bring them out into a wide arc and then down to the side of your body. As you breathe out, allow your mouth to come into a wide smile.

3 Repeat this four or five times, welcoming in the sunlight with each breath, before getting on with your morning routine.

WHEN TO DO IT

Every morning throughout the year. Make sure you get out into daylight, too. Try taking a half-hour walk at lunchtime. Be sure to do this in winter, to take advantage of the limited sunlight.

02 LEAN ON ME

Did you know that just by asking for help you could raise your self-esteem? Find the courage to allow others to help you through hard times, and you'll have it much easier than those who choose not to seek out a helping hand. According to emotional brain training, asking for support can help free you from a stress state. The next time you need support, use this exercise to feel cared about and recharged.

1 Take a moment to consider all the animal groups that naturally take care of one another, such as meerkats, elephants, and chimpanzees. These creatures instinctively groom one another regardless of who birthed them.

2 Try to think about all the emotional and physical support you've received through the years, especially when you asked for it or made it obvious that you needed help.

3 Close your eyes and imagine leaning on all those that helped you along the way. Feel a sense of deep security as you imagine others being the pillar to your soul. Now, one by one, see your burdens being lifted away.

WHEN TO DO IT

Practice this exercise every time you feel low or overwhelmed. Over time, finding the courage to accept support from others will make you feel more energized.

03 MOOD FOOD

Low self-confidence can be associated with poor eating habits, so make a good-quality diet part of the foundation of your life. The key thing is to have a balanced diet incorporating all the main food groups, but there are also several key foods that are especially good to include.

1 Studies show that people suffering from depression have low levels of vitamin B6 and other B vitamins, including thiamine (B1)—all of which are linked to mood and self-esteem. You'll find these crucial vitamins in protein foods, such as lean meat (especially turkey and chicken), fish, eggs, nuts, seeds, soy beans, and bananas.

2 An important nutrient for the production of the mood-enhancing chemical, serotonin, is iron. Sources include red meat, egg yolks, whole grains, nuts, legumes, and green leafy vegetables. Incorporate some of these into your daily meals.

3 Sugary foods give you a bolt of energy, but it's fleeting. Aim, instead, for foods that release energy slowly, which help stabilize your mood. Oats and lentils are perfect and both help with serotonin production, too.

WHEN TO DO IT

Healthy eating should be part of every day. Limit your intake of alcohol, caffeine, and sugar, all of which can adversely affect your mood and your self-esteem.

04 IF AT FIRST . . .

This exercise will boost your self-esteem when things go wrong. It is inspired by the emotional brain training tool of "damage control." Research shows that people with low self-esteem are troubled by failure, tending to exaggerate it, and focus on avoiding mistakes. As a result, they often bow out of a new challenge, depriving themselves of an opportunity to shine. Confidence means having the strength to accept that you will mess up sometimes, and that setbacks can be part of the journey to success.

1 Whenever you fail at something, acknowledge your disappointment. Just notice your feeling and verbalize it—"I am feeling fearful," or "I am experiencing disappointment."

2 Remind yourself that few people succeed without failing at some point. J.K. Rowling's first Harry Potter book was rejected 12 times before being published; Steve Jobs dropped out of college before he founded Apple.

3 Project into the future. Mistakes and failures can open doors to new opportunities; think how you might one day tell someone about this mistake or failure and how it led on to some great success.

4 Use visualization. Imagine you are trying to cross a fast-flowing stream. There's no obvious way across, but you can see there are a few stepping stones. You start to walk from one to the next— sometimes having to take a leap, other times having to step sideways or retrace your steps.

5 Remember that the path to success is not always straight on: Sometimes, whether willingly or not, you have to go sideways, even backward, to reach your goal.

WHEN TO DO IT

Whenever you feel a sense of failure or despair, or if you find yourself self-criticizing for having failed to achieve a specific aim.

05 POWER POSE

For an instant surge of confidence, look to your posture. A study at Harvard and Columbia Universities showed that adopting an expansive "high power pose" makes us look and feel more confident. Researchers found that holding the pose made levels of testosterone rise—increasing feelings of power—while making levels of cortisol drop, so decreasing stress. Take two minutes and give this exercise a try.

1 Place your feet at least hip-width apart, push your shoulders back, and hold your head high. Relax the knees slightly and let your weight drop into the lower body. Now curve your hands into loose fists and rest them on your hips.

2 Imagine yourself as a strong and powerful animal standing on its hind legs—a grizzly bear, say—and take strong, deep breaths. Feel the raw strength of this magnificent animal in your own frame. Do this for two minutes.

3 Remember this power pose as you go about your day and check in on the way you hold yourself. If you are slumping, push your shoulders back, raise your head, and breathe long and deep.

WHEN TO DO IT

This is a great exercise to do before an important meeting, or whenever you are feeling nervous or small. You can also do it daily, perhaps just before you leave home in the morning.

SEATED POSE

Claim your space when you are sitting too—keep your shoulders back and wide, your head up, and have both feet flat on the floor to help you feel stable.

TOP **FIVE** WAYS
to release your inner power

Listen to inspiring music

Look at an incredible view

Move your body: dance, stretch, wiggle, work out, walk briskly

Create: paint, draw, color

Laugh out loud for a full minute

06 FIT FOR LIFE

It is a fact that regular exercise helps increase your self-esteem. It releases mood-boosting endorphins in the body, and these make us feel more powerful and confident—a state dubbed "vibrancy" in emotional brain training. Research by the Eastern Ontario Research Institute found that people who exercised twice a week for ten weeks rated their body image and self-esteem higher and felt more competent socially and academically, as well as physically. Try these ideas to up your own vibrancy quota.

1 Get outside. Exercising in the open air is particularly good for boosting mood and self-esteem. Try heading to a park at lunchtime or walking a section of your daily commute.

2 Get moving for 30 minutes a day. Try to schedule regular exercise so it becomes part of your routine. Find an activity that you genuinely enjoy so it is easy to stick with it.

3 Expand your definition of exercise. Go square-dancing or join a tap-dancing class. Or get outside and garden. Even housework counts as exercise, provided you work vigorously.

4 Walk a dog. If you don't have a dog, offer to walk that of a friend. The University of Missouri found that dog walkers increased their speed by 28 percent. If you're not a dog person, buddy up—people walking with a friend or partner up their pace by about four percent compared to when walking alone.

WHEN TO DO IT

Being active is an integral part of a happy healthy life. If you spend a lot of your time sitting down, try setting an alert to remind yourself to get up and walk around every hour.

07 . . . AND RELAX

Sleep plays a key role in positive characteristics such as optimism and self-esteem. Many of us are so used to being stressed, however, that we find it difficult to sleep for the requisite hours. This progressive relaxation technique from cognitive behavioral therapy can help. It targets muscle groups one at a time to release physical tension and to disrupt the torrent of thought that blocks sleep.

1 Sit or lie in a comfortable position; once familiar with the exercise you can do it in bed, but while you are learning it is best to sit so you can concentrate. Take five, slow, relaxed breaths.

2 Start with your feet. The aim is to activate the muscles of the body, very gently and one by one, then to hold this tension for five seconds before releasing it again. Squeeze the muscles of your feet as if trying to curl them tightly.

3 Breathe in as you squeeze, let that breath out, and take another breath as you hold. Breathe out again as you let go. It can help to visualize the tension flowing out of your body like water from a spout. Enjoy this sense of relaxation as you breathe naturally for 10–15 seconds.

WHEN TO DO IT

Twice a day, morning and night, for two weeks. This will help you to become familiar with the exercise. After that, perform it every evening or whenever you want to relax.

LETTING GO

This exercise teaches your body the difference between tension and relaxation, making it easier to let go when you need to.

4 Move on to your lower legs; bring your toes toward you to activate the calf muscles. Now your upper legs; clench your thigh muscles. Do this on the right and then on the left, tensing and holding, then relaxing and resting.

5 Move on to your arms. Make a fist with the right hand and let go. Make a fist again and, keeping it clenched, bend your arm to bring the forearm toward the shoulder. Repeat on the left arm.

6 Tighten your buttocks by tensing the muscles. Pull in your abdomen at the same time. Now activate the muscles of the chest by breathing in deeply, then releasing. Next, draw your shoulders up toward your ears, before relaxing them back down.

7 Finally, bring your focus to your face: Open your mouth into a wide grin and release. Close your eyelids tightly and release. Now activate the muscles of your forehead by lifting your eyebrows as if you were very surprised. Release this final muscle group and rest.

QUICK RELEASE

Once you are familiar with the exercise you can do a quick version simply by practicing the releasing part. It's a handy de-stress exercise for work or home.

PERSONAL AFFIRMATION

I take time
to
relax
and
recharge

o8 A BRAVER YOU

This exercise makes use of a concept known as "fake it until you make it," often used by cognitive behavioral therapists. The idea is that, by acting as if you already possess a certain attribute, you begin to create a habit of it and over time it becomes second nature to you. Try this exercise and step into the shoes of a brave new you.

1 Get yourself comfortable in a quiet place— switch off your phone and ask anyone you live with not to disturb you so you can relax.

2 Consider how your life would be if you were naturally courageous and strong. How would you stand? What would you look like? What would the tone of your voice be like? Imagine a confident, braver you in as much detail as you can.

3 Now visualize yourself inhabiting the body of this brave new you—imagine yourself literally stepping into that person's shoes. What does it feel like to be in this body? Continue for as long as feels right before coming out of the visualization.

WHEN TO DO IT

Do this every day. It's an excellent exercise to do in the morning. Try combining it with repeating a positive statement about yourself: "Today I am the best I can be," for example.

09 START WITH A WIN

Your sleep-wake routine can set the tone for the whole day. Get up 10–15 minutes earlier than you need to and set yourself small goals that you can easily achieve. Starting the day with a sense of accomplishment puts you in the best possible frame of mind to achieve during the day. Try these ideas.

WHEN TO DO IT

Every day. Goal-setting is an important aspect of cognitive behavioral therapy, and meeting small achievable targets helps build positive self-esteem.

1 Prepare for the next day before going to bed. Sort your clothes, pack your bag, write a to-do list. Knowing you have what you need for the day gives you confidence and you'll sleep better for it.

2 Aim for at least seven hours sleep, so you wake up feeling refreshed. It's hard to tell yourself that you can take on the world if feeling groggy.

3 Make your bed every morning. This great mini task allows you to say, at the very start of the day, "job done."

4 Make time for something that gives you pleasure, such as coloring—a great way to introduce a small win into the morning.

Try this: Spend ten minutes coloring this pattern before starting your day.

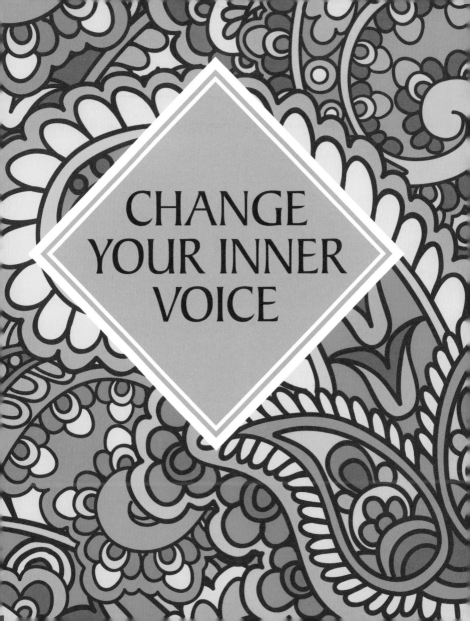

CHANGE YOUR INNER VOICE

The way we talk to ourselves can have a huge impact on our confidence. We all have an inner critic—a voice that magnifies our fears and our flaws, one that can become stronger and meaner the lower we feel. Negative self-talk can bring you down, sabotage your aims, relationships, and confidence. As a result, it encourages you to avoid taking risks for fear of failure, preventing you from embracing opportunities that may benefit your life.

Research shows that cultivating a positive inner voice—and using self-affirmations in order to do so—can boost your performance. Cognitive behavioral therapy, emotional brain training, and mindfulness-based stress reduction each offer ways to manage one's inner critic. By learning to speak to ourselves with gentleness and by treating our inner critic with humor, we can stop holding ourselves back and live the lives we want.

10 SPEAK KINDLY

What do you say to yourself when you forget something, have an accident, or make a blunder? We are often nice to others, but the ways in which we talk to ourselves can erode our confidence. According to cognitive behavioral therapists, our inner critic comes from an internal punitive master, a part of our consciousness that is strongly influenced by environmental rules we learned as children. To counter a ridiculing or mocking voice, it is important to find a more nurturing voice. Try this visualization to dismantle your inner critic and improve your self-esteem.

1 Think for a moment of a critical message you told yourself. Now try to neutralize it by thinking of how a nurturing parent would talk to their child about the very thing you blasted yourself for.

2 To help you adopt a more nurturing style of self-talk, consider writing down soothing, motivating, and esteem-boosting comments, just what any loving parent would say to their child.

3 Keep repeating sayings like, "It's okay, you'll do better next time," so that each nurturing message becomes embedded in your subconscious mind.

WHEN TO DO IT

Practice this daily until your inner critic is drowned out by your strong, nurturing parent voice. See how nicely you speak to yourself and how much better you feel as a result.

11 QUIET YOUR MIND

How much peace and quiet do you get in a day? Probably surprisingly little. We are constantly bombarded by noise, be it welcome or unwelcome. Emotional brain training specialists know that inviting silence into our lives is not only good for our health, but can restore our brain functions. Quieting your mind can help you reach your inner voice, creative nature, and emotional balance. Try this visualization to help your brain go into idle mode while you nurture the courageous part of your being.

1 Find a peaceful yet comfortable location to sit. Now close your eyes, take some deep breaths, and imagine your mind is going to the break room, or to "time out," a place that doesn't allow emotional turmoil or suffering.

2 Gently tell yourself, despite any random thoughts about your problems, that all parts of you are going to enjoy this moment of silence.

3 Encourage your pop-up thoughts to take a back seat in observance of silence. Imagine pushing away your mental problems as you go about your busy day, so creating a state of stillness.

WHEN TO DO IT

Practice this exercise whenever you feel that your thoughts are keeping your mind hostage. Over time, you will learn to invite inner silence and will be more in touch with your wise and confident self.

PERSONAL AFFIRMATION

I make space
for the
things
I want
and find it easy
to say "no"

12   LEARN TO SAY "NO"

Do you have "yes" as your default response when people ask you to do things? Many of us feel so uncomfortable saying "no" that we end up spending our time on things we don't want to do, and become burnt out or resentful. Here's a guide to the art of the negative.

1 Know your priorities. If you are aware that you want to spend time with your partner on the weekend, it's easier to say no to coffee with a friend.

2 We worry that people will feel angry or stop liking us if we say "no," and overcompensate with apologies or excuses. This can reinforce the idea that you should be saying "yes." A simple "No, that doesn't work for me" is much clearer. Keep your tone of voice steady and calm.

3 If you feel anxious or uncomfortable, notice the feelings and let them go. It is better to feel uncomfortable now than angry and resentful later.

4 Avoid worrying about what the other person will think if you say "no." In cognitive behavioral therapy this is dubbed "mind reading." Just notice the thoughts, and release them.

WHEN TO DO IT

Every day! Demands on our time can be unceasing. Be prepared to be persistent; some people struggle to take "no" for an answer.

13 TIP THE BALANCE

Try this "three compliments" tool to prevent negative thinking undermining your self-esteem. In emotional brain training, the aim is to break negative thought circuits in the brain and replace them with new, more positive ones. The exercise is based on the well-attested idea that the brain is malleable and can be trained away from stress responses, toward joyfulness and confidence.

1 Next time you notice that you're being overly self-critical, take a moment to pause and breathe. Do not berate or judge yourself for having the thought; simply let it be as you breathe.

2 Now find three things to say about yourself or your life that are truly positive and authentic. These can directly challenge your original thought, or it can be completely unrelated—the point is to replace the negativity with a mini-jolt of positivity. Allow yourself to feel the positivity by taking a conscious deep breath in and out.

3 You may like to imagine this as a pair of scales: Rather than letting your negativity weigh you down, you balance it out with three positives.

WHEN TO DO IT

As often as you can. The more you practice this, the easier the technique becomes. You may like to keep a notebook in which to write your compliments down. This can be a lovely thing to look through.

TOP **FIVE** WAYS
to nurture self-love

Look in a mirror and smile;
say "I love you"

Send yourself an email or letter listing
six things that you like about yourself

Ask three friends to
name your top strength

Make time to look after your
body and mind

Do whatever pleases you
every now and again

14 TEST THE HYPOTHESIS

Hypothesis testing is a powerful technique used in cognitive behavioral therapy, and can be helpful if you are fearful. The idea is to question certain assumptions. This can be particularly useful if you find yourself avoiding certain activities because you believe something bad will happen.

1 Identify the belief that is holding you back. For example, if you have an invitation to a party, but don't want to go because you believe that nobody will talk to you. Write down your belief on a piece of paper, fold it, and put it in a drawer.

2 Now test your belief—go ahead and do the thing that you are worrying about. If you feel nervous, remind yourself that, in this one instance, it doesn't matter what happens, because you are conducting an experiment. This can help to give you a little distance and make it easier to go through with your challenge.

3 You may well discover that your fear was misguided or inaccurate—people do talk to you at the party. When you have time to reflect, find the paper and look at the belief you have written. Write down what actually happened.

WHEN TO DO IT

Do this exercise when you have identified a negative belief that is proving an obstacle in some way.

15 GROW YOUR MIND

People can be grouped into those who have a fixed mindset and those who have a growth mindset. People with a growth mindset tend to be more persevering and less bothered by the success of others; those with a fixed mindset tend to give up more easily and resent others' success. Try this visualization to encourage yourself to believe you can learn, improve, and achieve—develop your growth mindset.

1 Adopt a comfortable position, sitting upright rather than leaning back. Take a few long, slow breaths. Close your eyes and bring to mind a seed. Imagine yourself planting it in the soil, watering the soil, watching the sun warm the soil.

2 Visualize that seed slowly sending out roots all around it, and then sending up a shoot. Imagine that shoot growing larger and larger, sending out small stems that unfold into tiny leaves.

3 Notice as your plant becomes stronger, its leaves growing larger, and then imagine one of the stems has a tiny bud upon it. This slowly grows larger and opens up into a beautiful flower. Enjoy its beauty for as long as feels right before slowly letting the image fade and opening your eyes.

WHEN TO DO IT

This can be a useful visualization to do when you want to cultivate an achievement attitude. Use it to remind yourself of the innate ability of all living things to grow and develop.

16 HUMOR IT

Most of us fear humiliation, and your inner critic can get louder and more unpleasant when you are about to do something challenging in front of others. The best way to beat this is with humor, which is a powerful weapon in the battle against negativity.

1 When you notice that your inner voice is on a loop of negativity, take a pause.

2 Picture that inner voice belonging to some comic and ridiculous figure—something that may be trying to be scary but fails because it is essentially laughable—a tough-looking pet in fancy dress or a soft "monster" toy might work here.

3 Give this creature or monster a ridiculous name—the Snaffgabbler, or the Snark, for example.

4 See that ridiculous creature repeating your negative words. It's harder to take them seriously, and helps to remind you that your fears and thoughts are not reality. And you may just be able to tell it to hush up!

WHEN TO DO IT

This is a good creative exercise to do when you are feeling calm, so that when you notice your negative thoughts, you can think to yourself "Here is the Snaffgabbler again," and visualize it as the source of these words.

CHANGE YOUR TUNE

A "can-do" attitude goes hand-in-hand with confidence. If you are plagued with nerves or a belief that you can't cope, then try this mindfulness-based exercise, which helps you to see your thoughts as a soundtrack playing in your head—one that you can change.

1 When you are troubled by negative thoughts, take a moment to sit down and close your eyes (if you are at work, you can do this in the bathroom). Visualize an iPod or CD player—whatever you usually use to listen to music. Picture it as clearly as you can, including the on/off button, the volume control, and the track selector.

2 Now imagine that those negative thoughts are emanating from the music device, just like a musical track. Then see yourself turning down the volume, and imagine that the thoughts become quieter as you do so.

3 Now visualize yourself using the controls to change the track. As you do so, imagine that you hear a new positive track. Try repeating the words "I am a strong and confident person."

4 Hear the new track for a minute or so, then slowly come out of the meditation and get on with your day.

5 You can distract yourself further from negative thoughts by giving your mind a more positive focus, such as a quick coloring project.

Turn the page: Try the coloring exercise overleaf to help switch negative thoughts to positive focus.

WHEN TO DO IT

Practice this exercise when you are feeling calm. Do it every day for two weeks and you will find it easier to switch off the negative thinking.

POSITIVE
FOCUS

You can become downcast when you focus on the negative—those things that you do not like about yourself and the imperfections in your life. You start to see the world as enemy territory and yourself as a victim of circumstance. By contrast, if you can train yourself to be aware of all the positives in your life, this will help you to notice what you have already achieved and how many gifts are present in your day. This change of attitude can cause your confidence and self-belief to soar.

This chapter offers you a range of tools and strategies to cultivate the positive—by actively searching for it, by practicing appreciation, and by taking the time to celebrate the small gains and triumphs that you might otherwise take for granted. The exercises that follow provide some important techniques to help you cut through the worry and boost self-acceptance of your unique self, flaws and all.

18   LET YOUR WORRIES GO

If you have a persistent thought or worry that is undermining your self-esteem, there are lots of techniques you can use to dispel it. Here are three great ways to let go of a worry.

1 Write the things that are troubling you on a piece of paper. Then destroy the paper by ripping it up, shredding it, or putting a match to it, if safe to do so.

2 Imagine tying a persistent worry to the string of a balloon, like a label, then let go of the balloon and watch it drift up into the sky until it disappears out of sight.

3 Schedule a specific time in the day when you can worry. Write it in your diary if you like. Psychologists call this "stimulus control." Use your worry time to think up solutions rather than just churning things over in your mind.

WHEN TO DO IT

These are if-and-when techniques, to be done as often as you need to. Sometimes worry can encourage you to sort out a particular issue, but chronic worry is a habit of mind—one that can be broken.

19 HAVE PATIENCE

Very few things in life come easily. We need patience and perseverance to put things we want into play. Real change is gradual, especially if we want to come out feeling positive, courageous, and accomplished. According to cognitive behavioral therapy, patience is a learned phenomenon. We can cultivate patience by observing the time and effort it takes to attain a goal. Consider this exercise in order to find and harness your patience.

1 Think of a time when you reacted with impatience. Looking back, do you feel a bit foolish for carrying on? Did all that fuss make a huge difference in getting something done? Ask yourself if it was really worth looking so silly?

2 Now try to see yourself at a much slower speed taking your time to accomplish that same goal. Notice how much more calm you feel as you reach the finish line.

WHEN TO DO IT

Practice this exercise whenever you feel rushed or pressured into getting something done. Over time you'll feel more relaxed and appreciate more fully the fruits of your effort.

20 EASY AS ONE, TWO, THREE

Expressing appreciation bolsters self-esteem. When you take the time to acknowledge what you have, what others do for you, and how much you achieve, then you are less likely to indulge in envious comparisons that sap your confidence. Try these techniques to up your appreciation quota of all the wonderful gifts in your life.

1 Write the alphabet on a sheet of paper. Challenge yourself to come up with something to be grateful for for every letter (when you get to X and Z, just find something that contains those letters rather than words that start with them).

2 Every night before you go to sleep, spend a few moments thinking of three things that you have appreciated in your day.

3 Set aside half an hour or so to write a gratitude journal—treat this as a meditation time. Sit and reflect upon the things you are most grateful for. Write about these things in detail, including any feelings that were triggered or anything that touched your senses—what you could smell, taste, see, and hear.

WHEN TO DO IT

Commit yourself to daily gratitude practice; focusing your mind on appreciation helps you to become more mindful, which also boosts self-confidence.

YOUR JOURNAL

Research suggests that a gratitude journal is best written weekly. If you prefer to combine this with your nightly gratitude practice that is fine too.

21 HAVE A BEAUTIFUL DAY

Whenever we do something kind for someone else, we can't help but feel confident—our levels of the feel-good brain chemical dopamine rise with a genuinely good deed. Emotional brain training experts say that acts of kindness are innate in all of us, but that the reward circuits in our brain shut down when we are overloaded with worry. The answer is to focus on the positive around us in order to jump start our attraction to natural pleasures. Try the following imagery to get in touch with the kind-hearted person you know you are and can be for others.

1 Take a moment to think about the emotional warmth you give others even when you yourself might be hurting.

2 Imagine that warmth to be that of the sun as it comes out after a cloudy start to the day. View your emotional stressors as the clouds that simply scatter with all your warmth.

3 Now think of something you'd like to do for someone else with your loving compassion. Make an agreement with yourself that you will allow your warmth to shine in the face of adversity.

WHEN TO DO IT

Practice this exercise every time you feel doubtful or frustrated. As you practice, keep in mind that helpful acts can scatter your negative emotions and leave you feeling gratified. You'll slowly observe how kindness is contagious and brings out the best in you.

22 BOUQUET OF PRAISE

How do you react when someone pays you a compliment? Many of us are self-deprecating, dismissive, or meet praise with sarcasm. Cognitive behavioral therapists believe this type of negative response is unhelpful, and it should be challenged and changed. Learning how to take (and give) a compliment gracefully is an important part of communicating authentically, and also helps with recognizing our strengths and boosting our self-esteem and confidence. Try this exercise to reset your responses.

1 Think of the last time someone paid you a compliment. How did you react? Write the compliment and your reaction down—use the checklist on page 77 as a guide.

2 Think about whether your reaction was passive, aggressive, or authentic:

• A passive response means you downplayed the compliment—for example, saying "Oh it was nothing really," when praised for a job well done.

• An aggressive response means you reacted negatively, with irritation or sarcasm—for example, "Well, that's what I am paid for."

• An authentic response is to accept and respond positively to the compliment without rushing to change the subject or return the focus on the other person—"Thanks, I enjoyed the challenge."

3 If you responded negatively, consider why. Unhelpful thinking patterns are usually behind this—we might feel undeserving of a compliment or believe that the person has an ulterior motive for offering praise. If you can, think of an opposing viewpoint for your negative thought—"I am deserving of this compliment," for example.

WHEN TO DO IT

This is a good exercise to do at home when you have some time to yourself. Practicing accepting compliments primes you to react positively when you receive them in real life and believe the praise that you hear about yourself, which can boost self-confidence.

4 Now imagine hearing the same compliment again. Take a breath and, in your mind, imagine yourself looking the person in the eye, smiling, and saying "Thank you. I appreciate you saying that." You may like to practice this in front of a mirror.

5 Visualize yourself on a stage, and imagine that one of your fans from the balcony throws you a bouquet of beautiful flowers. Catch the bouquet and look up at them. Imagine yourself saying "Thank you" as you give a wide smile.

6 Put this into practice next time you receive a compliment. Acknowledging a compliment in a positive way—and without trying to deflect the attention away from you—makes the praiser feel good. At the same time, it allows you to accept positive feedback and increases your confidence. Remind yourself to catch the bouquet.

GIVE BACK

Giving compliments is another way to practice authenticity. It creates positive interactions with others, which in turn builds confidence. Make sure the compliment is genuine. It can sometimes be good to tie the compliment to a question or conversation starter—for example: "I love that jacket, where did you get it?"

HOW DO I **RESPOND TO COMPLIMENTS**?

Use the table below to record compliments people have paid you and your reactions to them. Use the following key to tick the right boxes:

[**1**] Ignored it/changed the subject   [**4**] Dismissed/minimized it

[**2**] Disagreed and said why   [**5**] Responded with sarcasm

[**3**] Laughed nervously/said nothing   [**6**] Said thank you and smiled

COMPLIMENT	1	2	3	4	5	6

TOP **FIVE** WAYS
to encourage positive thinking

Use uplifting "can do" language

Instead of complaining, challenge
yourself to find a positive angle

Make a point of saying thank you
when people do things for you

Acknowledge all the ways you contribute
to the world and those around you

Read uplifting books and biographies,
watch inspiring films, listen to
upbeat radio shows

23 HAPPY SNAPPY

One route to inner change is to fill your environment with cues that incline you toward positivity and remind you of all the good things in life. Mindfulness teaches us to be aware of all the beauty in the world around us, but we can make a conscious effort to bring it into our surroundings too. Try this simple exercise.

1 Go out for a walk with the intention of finding something beautiful. It could be something you have never noticed before: an interesting door knocker; a plant growing from the cracks in the sidewalk; the smile of a member of your family; a sparrow perched on a fence.

2 When you find it, take a snap of it on your phone or with a camera.

3 Do this every day for the next week. Then make a point of printing out the images you have and putting them up somewhere you will see them often, to remind you of all the unexpected joys in the world.

WHEN TO DO IT

This is an occasional exercise to open your mind to the beauty of the world around you. You may like to make it a daily practice.

24 LINK UP

If you want to feel good about yourself, help others. After all, we are all joined to each other like links in a chain. Lift one link, and others are raised with it. Volunteering is a great way to boost your confidence and increase social ease. It also gives you a chance to try new things, contribute to your community, meet new people, and feel a sense of accomplishment—all of which can boost your self-esteem.

1 Find an organization or cause that you can believe in. It is more fulfilling to help a cause if you feel personally committed to it.

2 Do something that you enjoy or are good at. For example, if you love being outdoors, volunteer at a community garden; if you enjoy animals, consider helping at a rescue home.

3 Find out what's involved before you start—both in terms of the likely work and the amount of time you will be investing.

4 Have fun. Volunteering should be enjoyable. If it is not, then figure out why—is it the role, the time, the location, or the people? Be prepared to try something new if things don't work out.

WHEN TO DO IT

It's up to you, but don't overcommit yourself at the beginning—it is best to start with the minimum involvement and then build up gradually from there.

WISH OTHERS WELL

Lack of confidence is sometimes the result of believing that other people are better than us—smarter, braver, happier. This beautiful exercise can help you to rejig your attitude. It is based on a form of meditation called loving-kindness, which is often taught in tandem with mindfulness. Such practices can reduce stress and anger, while improving feelings of connection. They may also help combat social anxiety, too.

WHEN TO DO IT

Do this daily for two weeks and see whether your attitude toward other people shifts. Thereafter, do the exercise two or three times a week.

1 Take a few moments to sit calmly. Close your eyes and focus on the affirmation "May I be happy and safe." Say this a few times in your mind as you breathe naturally.

2 Go for a walk. Whenever you pass someone, say in your mind "May you be happy and safe."

3 Continue to do this as you walk along, whether a person is young or old, rich or poor, pleasant or unpleasant—just silently wish each person freedom from difficulty and pain as you pass.

4 After or during your walk, sit in a quiet place and close your eyes. Say to yourself "May we be happy and safe." Imagine your compassionate wishes emanating from you to all those around you.

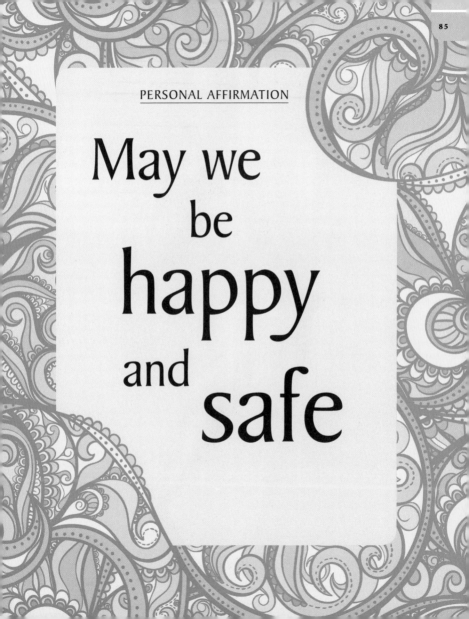

PERSONAL AFFIRMATION

May we be happy and safe

26 CELEBRATE A TRIUMPH

True confidence comes when you know your worth, and this self-affirming exercise encourages you to recognize all that you have achieved. Cognitive behavioral therapists use positive self-talk to help us notice and celebrate our triumphs, and to counter automatic negative thoughts that can damage our sense of self-esteem.

1 Sit or stand in an upright position. Take a few breaths to settle yourself into the exercise. Bring to mind something you have achieved recently. It can be anything at all—perhaps you cooked a meal that a friend or partner enjoyed, perhaps you met a deadline or solved a tricky problem at work, or perhaps you finally cracked how to parallel park.

WHEN TO DO IT

Do this exercise regularly—at the end of each day is ideal. Continue to celebrate your strengths.

2 Complete the sentence "I feel proud that I ...." Repeat this several times as you continue to breathe naturally.

3 Now imagine that you are holding a medal. This is your award for your achievement. Picture the color and shape of this medal, how it feels in your hands; visualize yourself lifting it up in triumph. As you hold your medal, repeat your sentence again, allowing yourself to feel the truth of your words.

27 FOLLOW YOUR LIKES

Could you imagine getting up in the morning and doing something you truly didn't care about? When we repeatedly do something we don't like, it has irreparable effects on our health and self-esteem. Cognitive behavioral therapists say that we are more inclined to have a happier outlook when we listen to our inner preferences and do something that gives us pleasure. Try this exercise to find what makes you feel prideful and happy.

1 Prepare your desk with paper and pens, paints, markers, pastels, or stickers. As you sit down, ask yourself what truly inspires you.

2 Take a moment and then let your hand draw it, write it, or trace it.

3 After each image, ask yourself again—what is your inner passion or what do you like. Then, again, create that image.

4 Keep creating images until nothing more comes to mind. Review the images you have created and take note of all the things you have identified as a source of pleasure. Resolve to make more time for these activities in your schedule.

WHEN TO DO IT

Practice this exercise once a week. Notice over time how much you gravitate toward the things you enjoy doing and how you look forward to doing them.

28 EMBRACE IMPERFECTION

Confidence comes when we accept ourselves, flaws and all. In emotional brain training this self-acceptance is one of the key reward states that make us feel good. Try this visualization when you notice yourself being self-critical. It helps you recognize that there can be beauty in an apparent flaw.

1 Close your eyes and breathe naturally. Imagine you are in a beautiful field of soft green grass. See yourself walking across the field, and imagine the breeze against your face, the natural aroma of the grass warmed by the sun, the soft springiness beneath your feet.

2 In your mind, find a place to rest. As you sit, you notice a patch of clover and run your hand over these delicate three-leaved plants. Your eye is drawn to one and as you look more closely, you see that—unlike the rest—it has four leaves.

3 Picking the clover, you examine it closely—the rounded shape of the leaves, its deep green color, the wonderful symmetry. It is different to all the other clovers, yet it is also perfect. You place it gently in your pocket as a reminder that you, too, are unique and perfect, just as you are.

WHEN TO DO IT

This is a lovely exercise to do when you feel you are different to others, or you feel isolated from a group.

29 KICKSTART CREATIVITY

"Get a hobby" may sound trite, but it's a great way to boost confidence. This is because hobbies, such as coloring, provide a creative outlet, while allowing you to find a sense of purpose. They also allow you to achieve what psychologists call "flow"—a state when body and mind are perfectly synchronized and you become totally engaged in what you are doing.

WHEN TO DO IT

Integrate a flow activity into your daily routine, as and when suits you.

USING MARKERS

If you are using markers in this book, place a sheet of paper between the pages to avoid the ink bleeding through.

1 Get your tools together in a quiet place. You can use markers or colored pencils—pencils give you more control and allow for better effects, while markers are brighter and quicker to use.

2 Take a few calming breaths before you start. You may like to close your eyes. Then select your first color—just choose one you are drawn to. Give yourself up to the fun of coloring, allowing yourself to experiment without judging the results.

3 Work for as long as suits you; if you haven't finished the design, that's fine—it can take a few days. When you do finish, take pride in your accomplishment by taking a photograph of it.

Try this: Color the image opposite to kickstart your creativity.

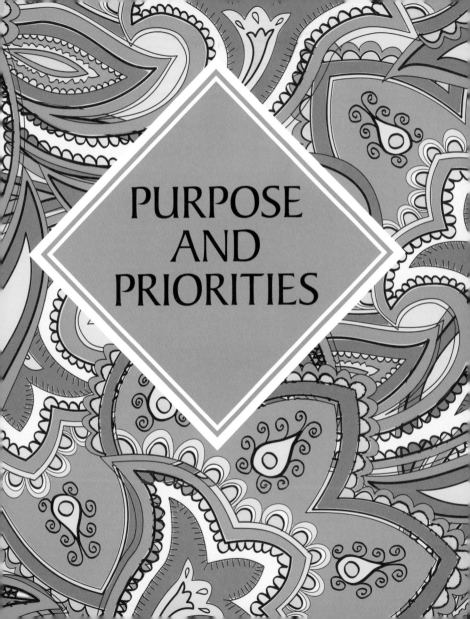

PURPOSE
AND
PRIORITIES

To have confidence, you have to have conviction. And conversely having conviction and direction can help to boost your confidence. Why? Because having goals, driving forward, and focusing make it much more likely you will achieve successes. And the more you achieve, the higher your confidence levels rise—it's a two-way street.

This chapter draws on a range of approaches to show you how to clarify your goals and take action to achieve them. True courage means venturing out of your comfort zone. This can feel challenging, and although worry and fear often block our way, they don't need to. In this chapter, we look at different strategies to cope with fear and prevent it from controlling you. You will also see how to use visualization to get in touch with your own inner strength.

Confidence often requires us to take action, but it's important also to make time to be still, and allow ourselves to connect with our inner truth. Understanding what we stand for, our truth, and our purpose not only enlightens us, but supports our ability to reach our full potential.

30 AIM TRUE

Having clear aims is crucial if you want to forge ahead in life. If your goals are unclear or vague, it is hard to focus and you are less likely to feel the sense of achievement that encourages you to persevere. Here are four evidence-based factors for successful goal-setting, drawn from cognitive behavioral therapy.

1 Be affirmative. Frame your overall goal as a positive rather than a negative. So, rather than opting to "stop eating junk food," start to "eat healthy food." People are more likely to achieve positive goals than negative ones.

2 Stretch yourself. If your goal is something easily achieved, it won't build your confidence—having an ambitious goal makes you work harder than an easy one. Think of it as an archer's bowstring—if it is too easy to bend, the arrow will not fly.

3 Measure it. Your overall goal should be so clear that an outside observer can see that you have achieved it. It helps to break down your goal into smaller steps, which should also be measurable: A target of "chat to two people I don't know at a party" or "make at least two points in the meeting" is easier to measure than "be more sociable" or "impress my boss."

4 Set a deadline. Telling yourself you want to get fit at some point in the future is too easy to dodge. Give yourself a clear timeframe—for example, "I will run a half-marathon in six months' time"—and then work out a plan for achieving it.

WHEN TO DO IT

Right now! Write your goal and vision for the future down. Writing down a goal helps to focus the mind and makes it more likely you will achieve it.

31 THE BIGGER PICTURE

People who dare to dream big find inspiration in all kinds of messages. Listening to a song can inspire us to write; reading can inspire us to learn something new. According to cognitive behavioral therapy, exposure to inspiring words or—better yet—the writing of them, can reinforce our desire to meet our goals. Taking pen to paper is like dropping a pebble into a pond; the more we write, the more we are empowered to keep writing as the ripples bounce off the shore and back.

1 Close your eyes and think of something you have always wanted to achieve or do. Now imagine that your index finger and thumb have the power to write words that remind you of staying focused on your goal, wherever you are.

2 Take out your imaginary tablet and try seeing yourself writing down a few of those single words that remind you of your goal. Say each word to yourself as you write it down.

3 Place the tablet in your imaginary back pocket and whenever you feel you need a refresher take it out, read those empowering words, and add a few more to the list.

WHEN TO DO IT

Practice this visualization whenever you feel your goal is becoming too vague or distant. Watch your inspirational list grow as well as the courage to reach your dream.

32 NEW FRONTIERS

Some people make sure that their lives contain as little challenge as possible. They may appear confident, but that can be because they are not testing themselves. True courage involves expanding your horizons. Try this visualization to remind yourself of that.

1 Get comfortable and close your eyes. Imagine that you are sitting in a beautiful garden, somewhere you feel safe and happy. Paint as detailed a picture of this garden as you can.

2 You see that there is a fence around the garden, with a gate leading out. As you walk to the gate, notice whether you have any feelings of hesitancy or expectation, even dread.

3 Take a breath and walk through the gate. Your surroundings are empty and barren. You walk toward a hill in the distance, and start to climb it.

4 When you reach the top, you are surprised to find a beautiful vista laid out beyond—with a river and grassy expanses, with trees and a distant village. There is a whole world to explore. You breathe deeply, happy to have found a wider world.

WHEN TO DO IT

This is a good exercise to do when you know your fears are limiting your potential. Do it every day for two weeks and see if you can notice a shift in your attitude.

33 HAVE A BUCKET LIST

Creating a bucket list is a popular way of cataloging the amazing things you want to experience in your life. You may already have one or two bucket-list items—by putting them on paper you can clarify your goals and develop a new sense of purpose in your life. Try this variation, which is all about taking your heart in your hands and challenging yourself.

1 Set aside half an hour or so to brainstorm your bucket list. Get a notepad and write down all the things that you wish you had the time and the confidence to attempt. Don't censor yourself. At this stage it doesn't matter whether your ideas are realistic or possible, worthwhile or utterly frivolous—all that matters is that you write down every single idea that comes into your head:

WHEN TO DO IT

When you have completed your bucket list, treat this as an ongoing project. Every time you feel inspired to do something new, simply add it to your list.

- to go white-water rafting
- to give a speech in public
- to learn the cello
- to ask a particular person out on a date
- to join a gym
- to whizz down a zipline
- to walk among bluebells
- to move to a new town

2 This is your first draft so try not to censor your thoughts—just keep writing, even if some of your ideas are ridiculous, impractical, or even impossible. Allow your writing to flow.

3 When you have finished, take a break. Come back to your list later, or revisit it the next day.

4 When you are ready, look at what you have written. Cross out anything that you truly don't want to do and refine each of your ideas to make it achievable.

5 Talk to your partner, friends, or family members about your bucket list. It can be a great idea to compare notes and team up with others to achieve certain items.

6 Write a second draft of your bucket list, then choose the easiest thing on it. Can you achieve it today, or take the first step toward achieving it?

7 Use the planner opposite to help you determine your steps. By focusing on the most achievable things on your list, your confidence will grow and you will feel empowered to keep your sense of priority and purpose.

MARK IT

When you achieve something on your list, make a point of marking it. Tick off the item, but also try writing about it in a special "bucket-list journal" kept for the purpose. Or have a noticeboard for pictures and mementos of your achievements.

MY **BUCKET LIST**

GOAL	MAKING IT HAPPEN
Who with?	1
Where?	2
When?	3

GOAL	MAKING IT HAPPEN
Who with?	1
Where?	2
When?	3

GOAL	MAKING IT HAPPEN
Who with?	1
Where?	2
When?	3

34 EMBRACE DISCOMFORT

If you want to be brave, you need to get comfortable with being uncomfortable. True courage means stepping out of the cozy zone. This mindfulness-based technique helps you just to "be" with fear—without being overwhelmed by it. Try it next time you feel worried, or stressed, or downright terrified.

1 Stop what you are doing and take the time to recognize the emotion that you are experiencing. It can help to name it—saying gently to yourself "I am experiencing fear" can somehow lessen its ability to overwhelm you.

2 Accept what is happening. You don't need to like what you are feeling; you simply need to acknowledge that this is what you are experiencing in this moment. Too often we resist or deny the truth of how we are feeling, but this resistance simply adds another layer of difficulty to our experience. When we allow our experience to be what it is, we often feel a greater sense of ease—and this acknowledgment takes some of the difficulty away.

WHEN TO DO IT

This technique is very useful when you are in the grip of fear or some other unpleasant emotion. Practice it on a regular basis, and you will find it easier to follow the steps when you are experiencing strong feelings.

3 Once you have accepted your experience, investigate it with gentle curiosity—what does this fear feel like? What is the strongest pull on my attention—my thoughts, a body sensation, or what? With an attitude of self-kindness, inquire as to what is occurring.

4 Do not judge what you are feeling, but simply explore it softly, gently. You may discover deep-held thoughts such as "I am not worthy" emerge, or perhaps that a body sensation increases in intensity. Whatever it is, and as much as you are able, explore it.

5 Realize that your feelings and emotions are not the same thing as you. What you are experiencing is an emotional state that has arisen, is present, and will pass in time. It can be helpful to use the formula "Fear is arising and will pass in time" or "In this moment, fear is present, but it will dissolve"—because this reminds you of the principle of non-identification.

6 When the emotion passes, take a few moments to breathe deeply. Consider whether there is anything practical you can do to support yourself in this moment, and do what meets your needs best.

SPOT CHECK

You may also find it useful to practice each of these steps individually. Stop what you are doing at random intervals during the day and check in with yourself: What emotion are you feeling?

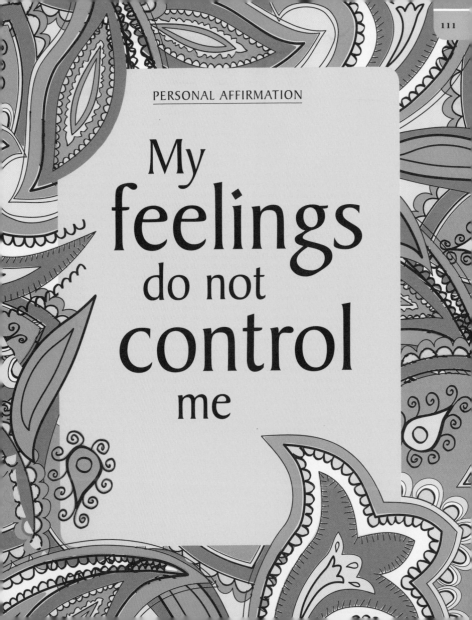

PERSONAL AFFIRMATION

My feelings do not control me

TOP **FIVE** WAYS
to keep motivated

Congratulate yourself on making
the effort, even when you
don't get the results you want

Forgive any slip-ups

Keep a monthly achievement log

Focus on what you can control, and
don't worry about what you can't

Make a point of hanging out with
positive and motivated people

35 DIVE IN

Try this visualization when you want to prime yourself to take a step into some unexplored realm, or to do something out of the ordinary. It's a wonderful way to foster a sense of adventure and confidence in yourself.

1 Close your eyes and get comfortable. Take a few long, deep breaths to prepare yourself for the visualization. Each time you breathe out, allow your body to release any tension.

2 Imagine yourself standing on a low cliff. Feel the heat of the sun on your head and body, and the hard flatness of the cliff below your feet. Look down to see the glittering aquamarine water. The water is so inviting. Allow yourself to feel the desire to jump off the cliff and into the water; but notice too, the fear of leaping into the void.

3 You step to the cliff edge and take a deep breath before jumping. It only takes a second, but you feel the breeze on your body as you fall through the air, and then the coldness as you cut through the water. You bob back up to the surface, exhilarated and refreshed. Take a moment to enjoy this feeling before coming out of the meditation.

WHEN TO DO IT

Practice this visualization daily for a couple of weeks to increase an ability to be decisive and take action.

36 TAKE STOCK

Does your mind go blank when you are asked about the totality of your life and where it's headed? If it does, then you are not alone. Most of us live a day-to-day existence and don't have (or make) the time to figure out what we really want to do next. Emotional brain training supports the concept of living our possibilities and being open to what else may be within our grasp. Taking the time to discover where you are in your life and what's in store for you is an important step in the process of self-enhancement. Try this exercise to build on what you have going with greater clarity.

1 Take a breath and, with pen and paper in hand, start sizing up your life:

- Are you living as fully as you can and if not, why?
- Where did you hope you would be in your life by now?
- When were you looking at making changes?
- What emotions or things are getting in the way of your dreams?
- Which resources are available to you right now?

2 Review the answers you have for each question and decide if there are any steps that you can take to move forward and make positive changes to achieve your goals.

WHEN TO DO IT

Practice journaling daily until you understand what is missing and how to go forward. Observe how your dreams will become more realistic and your confidence to accomplish more will become stronger.

37 MOUNTAIN OF STRENGTH

In mindfulness we practice staying steady whatever winds of emotion buffet us. This mountain visualization can be a helpful way of envisaging the strength and confidence that is inherent in your own nature. This strength can help you progress with courage at those times that feel the most difficult.

1 Sit in an upright position, so you are not leaning back for support. Take a little time to find comfort and stability, and to bring awareness to the breath as it goes in and then out of your body. You do not have to breathe more deeply or more slowly; just allow your breath to find its own natural rhythm.

2 Now slowly bring to mind the image of an impressive and beautiful mountain. Sketch in its large shape, the massive base being firmly rooted in the earth, and the sides narrowing to the tall peak.

WHEN TO DO IT

This is an excellent exercise to do when life feels uncertain and you worry about lacking control.

3 Slowly visualize your mountain in more detail— perhaps with a snowy summit, perhaps with pine forests or meadows cloaking the slopes, perhaps with glittering rivers and lakes. Enjoy making your mountain into a thing of awesome beauty, a monumental masterwork of nature.

4 Now imagine "bringing" the mountain toward you. It comes closer and closer until you and the mountain are merged as one.

5 You feel yourself as the mountain—your bottom resting on the chair or floor as the base, your body as the slopes of the mountain, your head as its peak. While you sit, breathing naturally, experience yourself as something that is as strong and stable as the mountain.

6 Broaden your awareness to the sky around you, and imagine that the sun is beginning to set and the sky is darkening. Notice these changes do not change the mountain that you are embodying. Allow yourself to experience the day and the night; the surface of the mountain may darken or lighten, the rivers may run into waterfalls or freeze over, animals may play, plants may grow, but the mountain remains the same in its essence.

7 Enjoy this experience for as long as feels right, changing the weather that batters the mountain—snow, hail, rain, scorching sun—and the life that goes on on the surface. But always know that the mountain's strength and essential nature remain the same.

8 When you feel ready, let go of the image of the mountain. Stay breathing naturally for a few moments and then slowly become aware of the sounds and feel of your surroundings. Open your eyes and take in the sights. Remind yourself that whatever a day brings, your essential nature remains the same, just like the mountain.

ENJOY SITTING

Take care of your physical needs when you practice meditation; spend time getting into a comfortable position and have an extra layer of clothing at hand (your body temperature drops when you are still for a long time).

38 FOCUS YOUR MIND

Confidence grows from competence, and the key way to improve your competence is to build your focus. Mindfulness of breathing is a simple effective way to do just that, especially when you use the "noting" tool. Here is the basic technique, which you can practice for a minute or much longer. It's a very simple practice that can be surprisingly challenging; engage a gentle inner voice if you find yourself becoming distracted.

1 Sit in a comfortable but upright position. Close your eyes and gently bring your awareness to your breath. Follow its journey into and out of the body by focusing your attention on your nostrils.

2 Notice the sensation of the cold air passing in, and the warmer air passing out. Imagine you have a tiny feather hovering on the tip of your nose. You have to focus very carefully to keep it there.

3 Your attention will drift toward thoughts, body sensations, or sounds. When you become aware of this, use the mindfulness noting tool: Label whatever the distraction is as "thinking," "feeling," or "hearing," and then gently direct your attention back again. Continue for your chosen length of time and then open your eyes and get up slowly.

WHEN TO DO IT

Every day for 5–20 minutes. Set an alarm so that you don't have to keep checking the time. If you are new to meditation, start by doing it for a single minute and build up the time slowly.

COUNT IT

If you are very distracted, try counting your breaths in rounds: breathe in, breathe out, one; breathe in, breathe out, two . . . and so on.

39 WASH AWAY

Confidence requires direction and focus, and one way to help build these qualities is to forgive your failures. A study at Wake Forest University showed that dieters who were encouraged to forgive their lapses, found it easier to get back on track than those who were not. So try this mindfulness exercise to stop the self-blame, and recharge your confidence.

1 Find a quiet and comfortable place in which to sit. Spend a minute or two breathing naturally, and focusing on the breath.

2 Bring to mind the event or action that you are regretting. Notice any reaction in the body, such as clenching or discomfort, and any thoughts or feelings that come up. Whatever these feelings are, allow them to be and keep breathing naturally.

3 Tell yourself that you accept responsibility for any negative behavior—"I accept that I lost my temper." Then consider whether there is any aspect of the event—such as the act of another person— that is not directly attributable to you, and say "I am not responsible for . . ." Is there a shift in your body sensations, thoughts, and feelings?

WHEN TO DO THIS

Try this exercise when feelings of regret or remorse are blocking your progress.

4 Now allow yourself to acknowledge anything you have learned from the experience, and anything you have already done to make amends or to help you to not repeat the behavior. Acknowledge your positive intention in doing this. As you continue to breathe, allow yourself to recognize whether there is more that you need to do and resolve to do it.

5 Gently tell yourself: "I forgive myself, and allow myself to start again," noticing and allowing any feelings or thoughts that come up as you do so.

6 Imagine yourself bathing in a beautiful river, allowing the flowing water to wash away any lingering feelings of self-recrimination as you do so. Repeat your words: "I forgive myself, and allow myself to start again."

7 To end the meditation allow the image of the river to fade in your mind, and then open your eyes slowly. Do something that nurtures and supports you, such as coloring.

Try this: Use lovely blues and greens to color the watery scene opposite.

DEEP FEELING

You may need to do this exercise several times over a few days or weeks, to allow the feelings of forgiveness to permeate your mind.

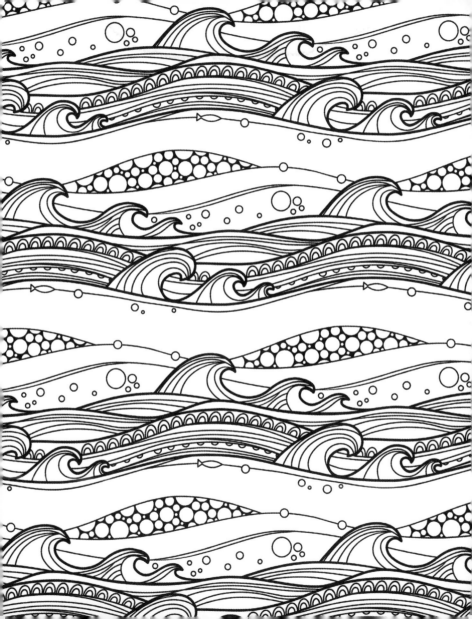

FACE THE
WORLD

Even the bravest of us can find that our courage and confidence desert us when we are in front of others. Fear of speaking in public is one of the most common phobias, and 75 percent of us experience it to some degree. Why? Some studies suggest that it's the idea of being judged by others that triggers our nerves. We all fear being assessed in real time, especially if we think there is a chance we might fail.

This chapter introduces a host of ways in which you can tackle the fear of public speaking—and communicating with others generally. The techniques are inspired by complementary psychological approaches. They include the rehearsal visualization tool, often used by top businesspeople and athletes (see pages 146–147); the elevator breathing trick from cognitive behavioral therapy (see pages 150–151); and theatrical methods for using your voice to convey greater confidence (see pages 154–155). Together, these approaches can help you to access the well of confidence that lies within you, so maintaining your equilibrium, however large or daunting the audience is that you are facing.

40 DO IT ANYWAY

How many times have you planned to do something, yet kept putting it off? We do this mainly because we have a fear of the unknown. Cognitive behavioral therapists postulate that change brings about challenges and it is up to us to think of problems as opportunities to conquer. Seeing difficulties as a chance to better ourselves can only result in more courage. Try these six steps to power through resistance and finally get things done.

1 Catch yourself reacting to life. Start monitoring what you are truly thinking and feeling.

2 Honestly appraise what you have achieved so far and stop beating yourself up about it.

3 Examine what has gotten in the way of change and find realistic goals.

4 Take note of your current commitments and assess what you can easily let go of.

5 Reframe your dream to make it more palatable, possible, and positive.

6 Remind yourself that trying is not doing and tell yourself, when all else fails "just get on with it."

WHEN TO DO IT

Practice this exercise daily until it becomes as second nature as brushing your teeth. Once in a while step back and notice how much more confident you feel.

41 TAKE A CHANCE

Being caught up in our own pain reminds us how much we need one another. When we are in turmoil, our mind has a way of eroding our confidence and telling us that we should suffer alone. Emotional brain training teaches us that all humans have an intrinsic need to be part of something greater than themselves. By applying the tools of intimacy, we can become aware of our need for loving compassion. Try this visualization to reach out to people you want to get to know and rely on.

1 Close your eyes and think of someone you may have met casually but want to know better. See yourself greeting them without a care in the world.

2 Turn your attention to something that they may have told you and ask them about it. Talking with them with ease may take some practice, but you are off to a good start.

3 Fast forward in your mind and imagine their support during a difficult time. Hear them boost you mentally and remind you that you are wonderful and will get past this rough patch.

4 Always feel inspired to reach out to new people who may be a valuable support in future.

WHEN TO DO IT

Practice this exercise daily before fully waking up in the morning. As you open your eyes feel more courageous and ready to reach out to someone of your choosing.

42   ANCHOR YOURSELF

This is a useful technique for inclining your mind toward positivity and confidence. The idea is that you can get your mind to associate a particular feeling with what's called an "anchor"—a small and very specific action. You can then "drop" the anchor in your mind when the need arises.

1 Think of a time when you did something new and unexpected. You may have been nervous, but you did it anyway. Perhaps you slid down a long water slide and found it exhilarating.

2 Close your eyes and relive the experience as vividly as you can. Bring as many of the senses as possible into your memory—what you can see, feel, hear, smell, even taste.

3 Bring your thumb and index finger together to make a circle and softly rub them together—this is your anchor. Continue doing this as you embrace the remembered experience.

4 Stop now and slowly open your eyes. The next time you feel worried about something, drop your anchor by rubbing your thumb and index together; the feelings should flood back.

WHEN TO DO IT

Practice often—every day if you can. The more you connect the action with a positive feeling, the stronger it will work as an anchor.

43 THE EYES HAVE IT

Maintaining good eye contact makes you look and feel confident. It is also key to connecting with others and building trust. People who are shy or anxious can find it difficult, but studies show that we feel mistrustful of people who don't look us in the eye, because it can also indicate lying. Try these ways to practice good eye contact.

1 Go out for a half-hour walk. During this time, try to make eye contact with at least ten people. Once you have made eye contact, smile.

2 Make a point of having eye contact with the person who serves you in a store or café—the general store checkout assistant, your local barista. Acknowledge them by looking into their eyes and saying "hi"; say "thank you" with eye contact too.

3 When chatting to someone, turn your body to face them square on—it is much easier to look them in the eye this way. Keep a mental note of how long you look them in the eye—we tend to maintain eye contact for three to five seconds—roughly the same length as an average sentence.

4 When listening to someone else talk, do the eye contact triangle—look into one eye for a few seconds, then the other eye, then look at the mouth. Keep following the triangle as they talk. This can make the other person feel "heard," especially if you also nod and make sounds of agreement.

5 Ask a partner or good friend to practice with you. Sit opposite each other and see how long you can maintain soft eye contact—the equivalent of the "who blinks first" game you probably played as a child. But this time, your gaze is soft and your aim is to connect. It can be very powerful and intimate.

WHEN TO DO IT

Try these tips on a regular basis—perhaps once a week—to help you maintain good eye contact.

SHIFT YOUR GAZE

If you find it hard to look someone directly in the eyes, try looking at a point between or just above them—they won't be able to tell the difference and it can feel less intense.

44 DIGITAL DETOX

Today we face the virtual world as well as the real one. There's much research to show that social media can encourage a comparison culture that undermines our self-confidence. In a recent study, half the participants reported they compare their accomplishments unfavorably with those of their friends when they go online. Mindfulness can help us to engage with social media in a more real and honest way so we can maintain a positive sense of self.

1 Before you log on, take a moment to relax your body and breathe. Check in with yourself: What are you feeling? Are you looking forward to seeing what your contacts are doing, or are you simply logging on out of habit? Observe how you feel.

2 Be real. Many people feel that they have to adopt a certain character online, but confidence means being your true self. If you can't be authentic, ask yourself what is the point of communicating online?

3 Join groups that make you feel good and give you something worthwhile. Disconnect from people who make you feel bad, just as you do in your everyday life.

WHEN TO DO IT

These are points to bear in mind every time you use social media. It's a good idea to refer to them at least once a week, to consider whether your online habits are helping or hindering you.

4 The online world can be fun, but it is rarely something that you need to be in touch with constantly. Beware the feeling that you are missing out if you don't log on and consider the fact that logging on will likely make you miss out on real life.

5 Avoid neediness. If others do not signal approval of your posts or comments, how do you feel? If you long for a response that you are not getting, consider whether your online interactions are undermining your confidence.

6 When you log off, check in with how you feel again—do you feel happier or grumpier? More confident or less? Social media can be a light relief, but it can also damage our feelings of self-worth. If it does for you, consider why you are doing it.

7 Set yourself limits—for example, avoid using social media first thing in the morning or last thing at night. Take a break to reset your thinking. In fact, give yourself at least an hour's window to engage with the reality of the moment and spend your time in the real world.

DEVICE-FREE ZONES

The easiest way to stop yourself accessing social media at bedtime and when you wake up is to make a point of keeping your devices out of the bedroom. Keep them away from the dinner table, too.

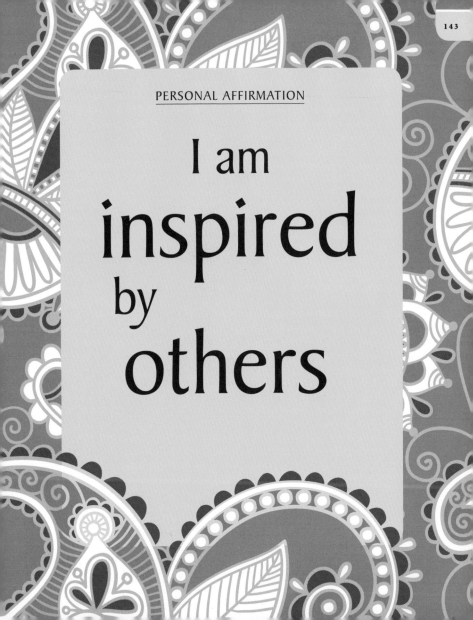

PERSONAL AFFIRMATION

I am inspired by others

45 BY YOUR SIDE

If you are doing something that makes you feel nervous, such as asking your boss for a pay rise or inviting someone on a date, try this visualization first to fill yourself with greater confidence. Visualization is often used in cognitive behavioral therapy because the brain responds to imagined scenarios in a similar way as it does to real-life events.

1 Sit comfortably in a quiet place where you won't be disturbed.

2 Close your eyes and bring to mind someone who evokes feelings of security and being cared for. This could be a parent, a much-loved pet, or an animal that you admire, such as a lion. Visualize this person or animal in as much detail as you can. Engage your senses in your mental picture: The touch of the person's skin or animal's fur, any distinctive scent, the sound of a voice.

3 Notice how good you feel when this person or animal is before you. When you feel ready, have them move to your side. Although you can no longer see them, you know they are there and feel that same sense of strength and support. Hold this feeling as you go to face your challenge.

WHEN TO DO IT

This is a good exercise to do regularly. By practicing it during times of calm, it is easier to access a loving presence in times of stress.

46 HAVE A REHEARSAL

Cognitive behavioral therapists stress the need to put in some preparation before you face the world. Creative visualization, rehearsing a favorable outcome, has long been used by top sportspeople and businesspeople to focus the mind. Try this imaginative exercise to prime yourself for a top performance—giving a speech, going to a job interview, or making a splash at a party.

1 Take a seat somewhere quiet, and bring to mind the event that you want to face with inner courage.

2 Imagine yourself in detail at this event. Picture the clothes you are wearing, the shoes, how your hair will look, the expression on your face—serious and collected, or glowing with happiness and confidence.

3 Now visualize this event going just the way you want it to. Imagine how interesting and charming you are at the party, how clear and persuasive you are as you talk to your boss, everyone laughing and clapping as you give your speech with effortless ease.

4 Bring the event vividly to life, as if it is a movie playing in a movie theater and you are taking the starring role. Incorporate as much detail as possible, using as many of the senses as you can—the sound of your voice, the applause, the heat of the spotlight on your face.

5 Play the scene back to yourself a couple times; the more familiar you become with how you want things to go, the more confident you will feel about getting started.

WHEN TO DO IT

Whenever your confidence needs a boost, and before important events.

BE PREPARED

Prepare in real life, too. For example, if you are giving a speech, make sure you know the layout of the room and have everything you need—notes, a glass of water, a working projector, and so on. Preparation is key to confidence.

TOP **FIVE** WAYS
to shine your light

Sit in the front row—don't hide at the back

Enhance your appearance:
Being well-groomed and dressing
well helps you feel good!

Come up with a one-liner that
sums up what's great about you
and repeat it to yourself often

Challenge yourself to say "hi"
to one new person at every function

Set your own standard;
don't compare yourself to others

47 ELEVATOR BREATHING

If you are nervous about speaking in public or to people you don't know, power up your breathing. Deep diaphragmatic breathing is a way of boosting your confidence. It slows the heart rate and calms you down, encourages good strong posture, oxygenates your brain, and even adds authority to your voice. Try this visualization.

1 Sit or stand tall with your head level and your shoulders back. Visualize your spine as an elevator shaft—with the tailbone as the base.

2 As you breathe in, imagine an elevator traveling up the spine to the head. Then as you breathe out, visualize it traveling all the way down again.

3 On the next in-breath, imagine the elevator traveling more slowly, just reaching the belly. Hold your breath for a count of three, then imagine the doors opening as you breathe out.

4 Breathe in and visualize the elevator rising to stop at the chest, again pausing then allowing the doors to open as you breathe out. Finally make it stop at the head, pause, then open the doors and breathe out. Repeat two more times.

WHEN TO DO IT

This is a good exercise to practice periodically throughout the day, as well as at any point you feel particularly stressed or nervous.

48 WIN-WIN CONVERSATION

Businesspeople talk about win-win negotiations, in which they respect the different perspectives and aim for a solution that everyone can accept. This philosophy can be applied to any sort of communication, and mindful speech can be a useful way of learning how to do it. When you adopt mindful speech, it means you converse with compassion, truthfulness, and awareness—and you listen too. Here's how to communicate with confidence.

1 When you are talking to someone, give him or her the full beam of your attention like a spotlight trained on a stage actor. Too often we are planning our next words while the other person is talking, so we do not hear what they say. And we talk before we have thought through our sentences. Make a point of taking a breath before you answer to gather your thoughts.

2 Try to maintain a connection with your beliefs while you are speaking, and speak authentically. Become aware of those times at which you say something to please or to fit in; it's hard to feel confident when you are molding your words to fit another's perspective.

3 Self-confident people can hear different opinions without feeling threatened by them. Focus on maintaining the relationship rather than scoring points, and try to understand the other person's motivations and needs.

4 Make a point of saying something positive (and truthful) about one person to another. Research has found that passing on an interesting fact about another person gave a slight boost to the speaker's self-confidence, while saying a mean piece of gossip actually made it drop (by as much as 30 percent).

WHEN TO DO IT

Whenever you communicate. Practicing mindful speech can transform both your communication and your relationships.

49 · SPEAK OUT

Developing an authoritative voice makes you seem much more confident to others, and it makes you feel more courageous on the inside, too. Here is a technique for helping you to project an assured and convincing persona by making the most of your voice.

WHEN TO DO IT

Speaking with a confident voice is useful in both work and social situations. Try out the tips next time you are talking with a friend, so you feel comfortable using them in a business context.

1 When you speak quickly, you appear less confident—as if you don't think what you have to say is important enough to give time to. So make a point of speaking slightly more slowly than usual. Taking a few long, slow breaths before you start will help (see Elevator Breathing on pages 150–151).

2 We can become very loud or very quiet when we are nervous. Speak loudly enough for people to hear you, but without shouting. Try slightly emphasizing the movements of the mouth to help loosen up the vocal chords as you speak.

3 Our voices become higher in pitch when we are nervous, so try slightly deepening your voice when you speak. Try practicing by talking into a dictaphone, and listening to yourself.

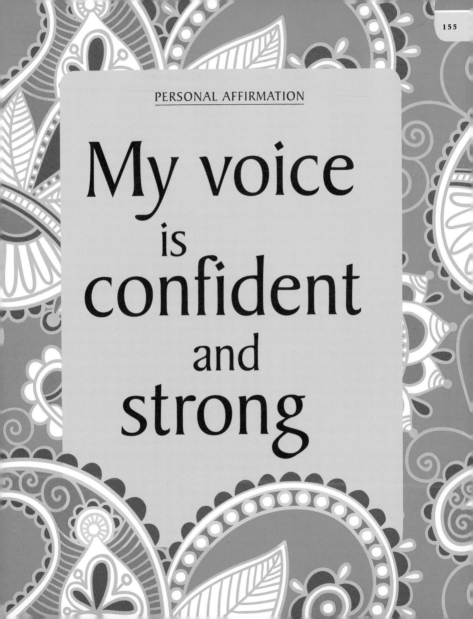

PERSONAL AFFIRMATION

My voice is confident and strong

50 COLOR CONFIDENT

There's plenty of evidence that what you wear can impact on your confidence levels. A study published in the *Journal of Experimental Psychology* found that people wearing a formal suit were perceived to be more powerful, and the way they were treated subsequently increased their own feelings of power.

WHEN TO DO IT

Every day. Taking care of the way you look is an important part of self-esteem.

1 If you work in a casual office, turning up fully suited might seem odd. Aim simply to dress one level higher than the average.

2 Grooming rituals—showering, filing your nails, brushing your hair, taking care of your skin—can give you a temporary confidence boost. It also signals to others that you care enough about yourself to think the basics matter.

3 Dressing in bright colors, especially red, can make you feel energized. If your job demands a sombre outfit, try adding a small detail of color—a bright watchstrap, an eye-catching tie or scarf, say.

Try this: Color this pattern using bold, bright shades.